A SOLITARY BLACK

Zak Aadam

ISBN: 1522823972
ISBN-13: 9781522823971

DEDICATION

Dedicated to Allah (SWT

CONTENTS

SHOUT OUTS

I'm not at the Grammy's but I'd like to take this opportunity to thank all the people who have supported me and given me encouragement and motivation. To all those brothers and sisters who kept asking to read my book. To all the brothers and sisters that gave me advice and have just been their amazing selves. Thanks for taking me to the mosque. Thanks for the invites and gifts. Thank you for your Qur'an.

I also like to send a big thank you to my mentor Abdullah at East London Mosque for taking the time to help me in his own time. You showed me great kindness and although I haven't seen you in a while it's because I had to finish a book. Now, I can get back to the Arabic Insha'Allah. Also big shout to Zia and the team at East London Mosque you guys do a great job trying to support the reverts.

Shout out to my revert brothers as well Abdullah who I met during an eclipse who has brought nothing but light into my life. Also Bilal who I met from work who is like my second conscience. I only hope to Fear Allah as much as these brothers.

Thank you to any Muslim who helped me to pray and

corrected my prayers. Big shout out to young rob, keep to the path my brother you'll do great things. Big shout out to Karen who I had the pleasure of witnessing a Shahadah in the fitting room also, at work.
Big thank you to my mum for just being there and being an amazing woman. Your strength is my dream. I hope we continue to become closer and I hope one day you'll love Islam as much as I love you. I have to also say a massive thank you as big as the ocean to the Girl in Black. Without your truth I would have lived a lie. Without your support I would have fallen. If it weren't for you I wouldn't have my new name. You've done so much for me that I can only hope to be able to return all the favors one day.
I saved the biggest shout out for last. That all praises and thanks go to Allah (AWT) who none of this, none of the air I breathe would have been possible. He is my greatest love of all. My apologies to anyone I've left out, it's like 2am and I'm tired. You are in my thoughts. Actually, I'm going to shout out anyone currently following me on instagram on the next page.

INSTAGR SHOUTS

M.I_LINES > _EYESEE_ > MRTEEJ7 > S_AAX >
RECHARGE_YOUR_DEEN > ANWRITES > SOULWRITTEN >
I_AM_MAZ > REZWANAAAA_ > MOHAMMEDHARUN23 >
TASNIAAKHTAR > MAKEUPBYSHANAZC >
SIMPLEREMINDERS > HTTP.NXRA > MUSTAAKK >
RESHMA___ > SAMYISLAM > RESHMANASRIN__ >
MANALABDALLAX > SENYAA_ > _SULTANA.AB > SHUMINA_
> SNASHREN > DEBORAH_DELGADOO > N_A_Z_I_A_ >
_R.B_X > SABIINA_X > AISHAGANI > ABZZII786 >
AHMODALI > NEELACHRONICLES > ABEGUM70 >
MUSLIM.UKHT > BRUNIAZLNIEVE > CKC_92 > DAPPERLDN
> SFABS_ > F4MMO > ___._X > I4HD > FARID.ROCKY >
FYZ_A_ > GAJENTHAAK > JELLYBEAAN > HAMIM786 >
MOGHULARTS > HAZERAA > HUMAYUNRC >
MOHAMMEDISA > MIZZ_JAYKAY > JAYJBELL > JEEVA_38 >
CHEJESSE > JUBERHUSSAIN1 > JUNED_07 > KIEFER20_ >
K.KINOO > _KSAHMED > SILENT_STRANGER >
ANOTHERBEGUM_ > MARIO_MO > CUBEZYY >
MIZANUR_RAHMAN_94 > IISMOMO > AHSANURKHAIR96 >
MOALI92_ > MOHAMMEDHAIDER91 > MUSLIMSPOTLIGHT >
HAZEYY_MUSTAK > SOULTOBLEED > BYNAJMAH >
ISLAMREVET > M6R4D > _ZA.95 > MHRN.X571 > A0606KA >
YAMEEN07 > NABEELABHABHA > RAJ.A1 >
SANIATHEPANDA > SAMIRA_AA7 > _RUBINA_B > RAASH_I>
RH.POETRY > NASRIIN_AKTAR > PRIYANKA_ARORA1 >
MINARET_BOOKS > SHADESOFHERINK >

4EVERYOURUKHTI > SYEDASHAH110 > _ADORINGALLAH_ > MUSLIM.PATH > SIRFMENA > HALLA_1978 > MODESTPEARL > MUSLIM_SPORTS > MOTHIUR105 > FEESA_H > OLIVERTHEAUTHOR > NEIMOASKAR > PUJABORDHAN > QARI_BROTHERS > UMM.SULEYM > SALMANAZIZ91 > MUZNAWRITES > FOREVER.PRINCESS_1998 > ITSMEMAN_

INTRODUCTION

It's been a year and nearly a half since coming to Islam. I've been asked what my story is. Someone usually says, "Do you mind if I ask you a question?" I know what's coming. I like that people ask, but I've told it so many times I can't do it justice. So, I decided to write it down and say everything I feel that I have to.

We are all made of a story. Our pages are inked with a permanent black. The white remains behind the dark colour to remind us the light is always there. The pages turn and the chapters of our lives pass us by until we reach an end that we ourselves will never be able to read. I am in the middle of a story. My journey to Islam has been my entire life. I was predestined to type these letters as if Allah had written them for me with His own pen years before I was born in St Thomas's hospital in Lambeth. Before I was raised to single parent mother in Clapham without a father, brother or sister.

In all my years there are some parts of my story I remember more than most and there are others I feel should remain within me, for now. Before Islam, my chapters were dark, mostly because I lived in the night. These experiences, pains, confusions and loss made me appreciate life so that I would be ready to appreciate the benefits of faith when it came. I had to feel lost to feel found. I had to feel heartbreak to feel real love.

For you, I will select a few nights from my life before Islam and a few mornings after. As I wrote this book I could see how much Allah has brought me through to reach the other side of the tunnel. There is always light when you turn to it. In the nights, my friends called me RawDeal.

PART I. SLEEPLESS NIGHTS

CHAPTER 1

Underneath a solid black metal door to the council estate roof, we'd come as far as we could before my cousin Suicide, took out a long black crowbar from his black jacket. Standing beside him with his long plaits we're the same age, fourteen. We're both tall, slim and with caramel coloured skin, but I have a clean haircut in my blue Adidas tracksuit. Looking down the hallways left and right there is nothing but washing lines, some rubbish and bits of furniture either way. The midnight hours kept everyone inside. Everyone but us, the night kids. Standing on the top of the stair rail he breaks open the padlock of the metal square. It hits the ground no longer needed in this world having met a stronger force that broke its will.

On the rooftop of the council block, there is a landscape of night sky lit with a skyline of lights and rising smoke. Over the city, we are still under the sky full of dark purples and oranges chasing clouds from the streetlights. Red brake lights and white headlights run from each other on roads beneath. Where are all the people going? I always wonder when I see traffic where there is for all of us to go. To them, I am just traffic to. Another passing soul never to be seen or recognised again.

The air is calm and nothing blows around us as much as a gentle caress. Suicide walks over the gravelled rooftop toward a tall antenna sticking up. He goes to work on it. We needed an antenna for his pirate station On Top FM. Back then pirate was getting as big as mainstream radio. More street kids less mainstream music. Voices from the ends ringing through illegal airwaves. Who has a right to say they own the air?

As he wriggles with the antenna and I can't help but admire him for his purpose. He wants to get it for his dream of running a big station. I just see a piece of metal. I have no purpose of my own. There is nothing that willing me in this world. I am simply watching the clouds drift over me waiting for lightning to strike or rain to fall. There is nothing I know I want except to be outside and to see. From the roof, the world looked a little bigger than my road in Clapham or Suicide's block in Stockwell. I like it up here. Above the drama, above the problems. Nothing can touch me up here accept the clouds and they are far away.

The peace of my thoughts is broken by the sound of the snapped antenna. Returning the way to the square, our trainers crunch the gravel. Mine are an inexpensive pair of reebok classics with shiny stripes. The hole we came up through is black. What are we going back to? Why can't we stay here among the skyline? I take my time before bidding a farewell to the roof above the chaos. This is a place I want to keep somewhere in my heart.

We leave through the black hole back into the drama. Back into the grey, back into the dark like shadows diving into a lagoon at twilight. I didn't know what Islam was then. I was a million miles and over a decade away the peace of the skyline.

Removal men

I'm thirteen hanging on the side of a white window of a council estate flat. "He can do it." Said a low voice from behind me. Without knowing why I was asked or how I got here, I kick in the window of a Stockwell estate council flat without breaking the glass. Under the cover of purple night and street lights, I slide my way into the empty flat while the boy's wait outside. I'd done it, and I feel a satisfaction at succeeding even if it is breaking and entering.

Inside the flat, the white walls reflected dim lights and angled shadows across the kitchen as I step down off the sink onto a wooden floor. The flat was unfurnished except a white fridge. Walking through the empty space ghosts watch me hiding behind the walls scared of the intruder. Opening the front door, the boys entered. There was only one that I actually knew. Suicide, my cousin. Not my real blood cousin, but when you'd known a kid a while they became family just by the amount of time that's passed. He grew up in the block, I came to visit. The other boys were older, in their twenties or thirties, I couldn't tell because their hats were so low and the night so thick.

The older boys carry out the fridge like removal men navigating the hallway, the door and the two staircases out onto the street. It's then that I start thinking who the fridge belonged to. That someone is going to come home and find their fridge missing. Walking around carrying this fridge the older boys don't seem to know what to do with it. I am hanging around the block with my friends just waiting as they disappear into another block. My cousin and I just there waiting around for the next thing to happen. On pause. We weren't worried about police for some reason. It was like they didn't exist until you saw them.

After ten or fifteen minutes the older boys come back with the fridge. They carried this block of white ice around the streets with nowhere to go. I don't know if they had someone who wanted to buy it or not. I hear one of the boys say it's getting hot so they take the fridge back up the stairs, back into the flat and leave it. What was the point of all that?

When I was born my mum moved from the block in Stockwell just a road away in Clapham because she knew what it was like here. Growing up I wasn't on the block, not until I reached secondary school age and started hanging around my mum's old friend from the block's son. Suicide.

The blocks opened up a world for me. I had a taste. After a few mouthfuls, I put down the knife and fork because no one at the table looked like they were happy. Didn't matter how much food was on their plate. It wasn't for me and I knew that from the beginning. Back then I was always a moment away from ruining my life. It is funny how just a few roads can make all the difference to your destination.

Black Icarus

Fifteen years old I climb out of my window at my home in Thornton heath. In my Adidas hoody and tracksuit bottoms. My laces are loose, there was no time to tie them. Pushing back the window glass I free myself as the heavy knocks on the front door send a tremor up the stairs. Out of the window, I fly into the moonlit night like a crow leaving my room behind with my weights spilled across the floor where mum tried to pick them up. They rolled slowly across the floor as she tried to throw them at me.

On to the roof of the conservatory, the tiles are loose but I steady myself with my wings. Down and over the back garden passed the stolen red moped I scurry into the road behind the house. My wings carry me so fast wind breaks like glass all around me.

Looking behind me I see a policeman, wide and stubby running after me as best he can but I am way ahead of him. I am flying and he is just running. There is a black desert between us of tar and white lines dividing the road. Huffing and pulling every muscle I can feel his efforts while I glide passed the parked cars into the night sky. I am underneath the moon flying higher and going faster until the air becomes hard to breathe.

All of a sudden my feathers start to fall out and I can feel a stitch in my side. My burst of speed is coming to an end, why can't I fly forever? Dam this human body. The roads I live on are so long and straight there are no short cuts to take between the houses. My sides are burning and my adrenaline is draining away. Falling from the midnight, I leave my feathers flowing away from me into the moonlit sky where I wanted to stay. My breaths are so furious and my body screams at me, begging me to stop. So I duck down by a nearby car and lay underneath it by the curb.

Moments pass over me as I try to gather my loud breaths back into my mouth. They keep coming out of my burning lungs. A pair of black boots steps into my view underneath the car on the other side. Staring at my breaths, I beg them all to keep quiet and to hide behind the tires. Everything is silent. The boots are paused on the other side. "Come out." Said a booming voice. He wouldn't have been able to catch me if I wanted to fly again, but I had nowhere to go.

Being booked in at the station the police talk among themselves about mum. She had given the policeman an earful that she didn't want me back that night and I had to stay in the cell to learn my lesson. The policeman looked at me with pity as he ushered me through a hallway of metal doors. A cockney voice scratches its way out of one of them. It's a man swearing, complaining about something or other. I keep quiet. There is nothing to say. Sometimes you just have to accept your fate and mine was behind a metal door. The policeman puts me inside a small room. It can't even be called room really, it's more of a box with an uninviting plank sticking out of the wall that must where I sleep. There is a tiny silver toilet in the corner I don't want to go near. A pale light shines through a small thick frosted glass in the wall. It couldn't be called a window because you can't see out of it. This was more like a glass wall in a brick wall. The door shuts behind me and I feel the weight of it.

You are drawn to what is the most comforting thing in any situation and for me, it's the plank. The cold floor would be my second choice, but I choose the plank by the window preferring something that resembles light, and something that resembles a bed. Sleep is the furthest thing from my mind as I go over the night in my mind in a flashback to figure out how I got here.

I can't remember how the argument started at home, I and mum were arguing as normal, but, this time, it is different. She tries to throw my weights at me and when that fails she puts her hands on me. This time, I hold her wrists pushing them away from me. It was the first time I'd stopped her from hitting me. In her angry eyes, she could see I wasn't her little boy I was six foot tall and I wasn't going to be struck anymore. Not by her not by anyone. I'd always said in my mind from when I was young that one day I won't just lay down and take a beating. What now? Well, she calls the police and tells them I'm vandalizing the house, which I wasn't. Looking at her lie down the phone is one of the most disturbing experiences I've ever had. When people feel they've lost control they become mad but control was never the answer.

I'm in my cell and despite going over and over it, there are times when you just can't believe how out of hand a situation has gotten. For the first time ever in my life, I'm bored out of my mind. Being an only child, I'd always find ways to entertain myself but in this cell, all I can do is count the bricks to pass the time. It was that night I knew I had to avoid jail if this is what it's like. You take for granted the fact you can just walk out of a room when you feel like it. When you're thirsty you open the door and go downstairs for a drink. When you want to go to the shop or meet friends you open whatever door you want whenever. I never wanted to be locked up again.

Sixteen Years

I'm sixteen sitting in a wooden cabin in the woods somewhere just outside of London. There are a few other kids around me. A few boys and one chubby white girl. The three other boys are all trying to get her to give them head, but she only likes the boy who isn't interested.

My phone rings through my pocket. It's a small black brick of a phone the same as every phone around the millennium. It's Suicide, he needs to talk. Outside the cabin, the night preys on the forest leafs feeding on their green shades turning them dark blues. They cross over me showing only glimpses of stars far away like small lighthouses beyond an oceans sky. There isn't anyone around me. Nothing except sweeping gusts gently hovering over grass and fallen leaves laying on the bed of the forest asleep. Suicides voice is the loudest sound in the forest. His voice is slow. The air wisps but it's not cold. He tells me our friend is dead. Stabbed in the heart by a mad man in Peckham in the middle of the street. He bled out into the tarmac and there was nothing Suicide could do as his life passed through his skin drifting into the air.

It was Tallman. Tall, dark-skinned, skinny, loud and full of jokes but you wouldn't mess with him. He was only sixteen, just out of school. We met when Suicide brought him to my school to break me out of lessons. We'd bunk off and cause mayhem around the town. Nothing sinister, just jokes. He led us into an opticians store once. We all went in without any money and left wearing designer glasses. I'm not sure if the shop staff new or just didn't want any trouble. We wouldn't have done anything violent, we were just having a laugh. It was funny at the time he was the funniest of all of us. He was…

The forest is a quiet and still place. A leaf on the ground beneath me awoken by a single tear falling on it. It's hard to think of someone who is in your mind as never being there again. You think back to the last memory you had of them and you can't believe it will be your last. Death is so commonly known yet it's always so sudden. This is all our fate yet when it picks us from the earth we can't believe it.

There I am in the forest trying to make sense of it. This is the life we choose. To be out at night among the madmen and the hoes. Turning the phone to my side after a solitary and swift goodbye to Suicide I stand in the dark wondering what just happened.

Walking back over the leaves rustling under my trainers I go back into the cabin and tell the youth leader I want to go home. I had been on a princes trust retreat for let's say, misguided youth after being kicked out of my first college after only four weeks. I didn't really want to be here anyway, I'm not that comfortable among strangers and I just want to be alone. Alone with the voices of my mind.

CHAPTER 2

Hostel Girl

I'm seventeen sitting in my hostel in Croydon wearing my South Pole grey hoody. I wore it everywhere even in the blazing hot summer. The room is at the top of the hostel and the ceiling is a loft. There is a sink by the wall over a square patch of wood where the carpet had been cut away. The walls are a dark and cold grey.

My mum had enough of me and threw me out. This time with a letter I gave to the council saying she wouldn't take me back under any circumstances.

It's a late and everything is quiet except for the shuffling paper across the bed as I write my rap lyrics across torn out pages across the floor. All of a sudden there is a knock at the door. The door opens because it wasn't locked and in pops the head of a small Indian girl. Maybe Pakistani about sixteen. Her hair isn't flowing, it's in a kind of ponytail but gelled down at the front. I don't know why girls glue and wipe down the front of their hair to their forehead. I'm always scared to touch it in case my hand gets stuck.

She had moved here just a few days ago. Wearing double denim and a pink vest she comes into my room and sits on my bed. Wondering why she is here there isn't much, we can say.

We're two lonely outcasts finding a time and place in the darkness to not be alone for a few moments. She feels broken, empty and lifeless. I know because I do as well. There isn't anything about her I like or know, but she undresses anyway. Looking over her I don't feel anything. A few moments pass in passionless silence then she just gets dressed and leaves. I'm glad nothing happened because I don't have a condom. I knew I would have done whatever she wanted if she persisted, but I think she came to realise she didn't know why she came either. That's what lonely girls in the ends do. They come to you thinking sex is the answer to their emptiness. It never is.

Raising the Bar

In my room at the hostel, I'm unscrewing the twenty kg weights set while the light bulb barely reaches the corner of the room I'm kneeling in. Picking up the bar I let the metal discs drop to the floor. The bar is solid hard iron and I grip it tightly. There's no way I'm going to let that boy think he's top around here. I don't know where I'm going to hit him, how hard or how many times but I'm going to.

Down the unlit stairs to the landing of the hostel's first floor, I can hear his voice coming from inside fat boy's room. At this point, I'm on auto pilot. Opening the door to the room there he is on the other side talking to some fat boy. A fat white kid wearing a new era cap smoking weed. The mixed raced boy I'm after looks at me then looks at the bar. He's wearing his grey sweatshirt and track bottoms.

About a year older than me and wider. Moving like I'm the terminator, I walk over to him a few steps and lift the bar back. As I pass the fat boy I stumble and the mixed-race boy grabs my arm. Trying to wrestle it back from his grip I can't, he's too strong for me.

Fat boy is just staring at us holding his spliff while this boy and I wrestle over the bar. I can't get it off him, but I can't let him have it either. We wrestle with for what seems like an eternity. I tell him "let go." And he tells me "you let go." None of us are letting go of this bar. So what do we do now?

In the hallway, we move up the stairs on step at a time toward the hostel officers room both still holding on to the bar looking at each other all the way. We've decided the best thing to do now is get someone to take the bar off us. A third party, a mediator. We move slowly, one step by one step both of us not saying a word under our heavy breaths like we're carrying a bomb.

What is going on and how did I get here? It's like I was drugged and the drug was called stupid, but it's worn off and I feel like a dick.

We get to the top step where the hostel officer stays waiting for him to answer our shouts to wake him up. Out steps this middle-aged white man with fading hair looking at two boys standing outside his door holding a metal bar.

Earlier that night I'm in the communal room. There's a thick glass door leading into it with panes of glass cased in heavy wood. Every time someone new would come to the hostel you'd see them through the glass. I'm sitting in my south pole hoody wearing my crew's chain watching television with a few of the other hostel. A new boy has come to the hostel He's tall and mixed race with thick arms. He must have been high because out of nowhere he starts talking nonsense to me. He walks over and stands over me casting a shadow on my face while I'm watching the TV.

He is too close. My personal space is tightly wrapped around me. Ignoring his stupidity he grabs my chain and flicks it on my chest. That was it. That was the reason I wanted to bash his head in with a metal bar. It was disrespectful and I wanted to teach him a lesson. Words never meant much to me then, the easiest answer was violence.

It was less than two months after arriving at the hostel that I would almost have unprotected sex with a random girl, and possibly go to jail for caving in the skull of a random boy a few days later. In those moments, my life could have been ruined. The next day I would be kicked out the hostel. Thank God. Who knows what would have happened if I stayed.

Back from Brighton

Carried through tunnels over tracks far away from home the future is the last stop. If I could keep travelling on this train I would. Wherever it would go I would stay here without my ticket and look out the window. Passing by the night skies as a blur of dark oranges over murky greens of fields and grass I'm flying through time. If this carriage would keep moving I would be far away from the voices shouting after me to leave. All the drama can stay behind me if the train keeps going. Everything I leave that isn't a heart for me can be forgotten. Why must this train have the last stop?

As the train pulls into Brighton and I'm eighteen. The only thing I can do is keep going straight. Over the barriers with a single jump before I ever heard of free running I land on the other side of nowhere in particular. Leaving the station, I am greeted with a lack of direction. Whenever I don't know where I am I always go straight until there is no straighter and I have to turn. Outside of the station, I follow a downward slope into the night with people walking around coming in and out of bars.

The concrete spirals toward a parting between the buildings showing a sky coloured in from the bottom with a moving mass of black. Closer and closer I walk pushed by the breeze until I can feel the waking cold of the oceans air rising over the peer flooding the street. The ocean is straight ahead. As I came to the peer I look out across the thick blanket of moving silk. Looking out, I had reached the end destination. Wishing I could keep going this is the last stop, the sea would surely swallow me. Would anyone ever notice? What now? I couldn't go straight anymore so I turn left and walked alongside the ocean as if it were accompanying me on my journey. The very weight of the waves coming to shore has so much power and peace in their crests. Side by side we walk, strangers in a new town I'd never been to before telling each other secrets.

The ocean said a farewell to me as its breeze pushes be up a hill. Where was I going? I had chosen and new straight and I did not know what the last stop would be. I'm flanked by suburban-looking houses the further I go. The night has become thicker and the streetlights less often. Behind me, a family of them watch me go on into the mass. The roads are so quiet, not like my high-street back home in Thornton heath. My mum was surely asleep by now, none the wiser where I'd gone. I can't even remember what we argued about this time. The road winds and twirls around houses until I come to a complete black. No longer can I see down the road. There are no lampposts, street lights or house lights. Standing in front of complete darkness I can go no further. This was the last stop. There is only so far a man can keep travelling into darkness before he misses the lights of home. This time, I wouldn't look for another straight. Back where I came from was the only direction I could go.

Going back the way I came I wanted the lights of the

town where I could see. My feet are tired and they need to stop walking. There is a black bench among the lights of a town in a park. Through the trees behind this park is a building lit up with purples and reds shooting across it. It looks like a Taj Mahal. I don't feel to go anywhere near it. Laying on the black bench, I see men in the distance walking into what looks like a gay club with a bright neon sign.

There is no future in my heart, but I can hear the voice of the ocean keeping me company through the town. Through to the park and passed the trees I don't feel as alone as I should have with the ocean still near to me. My eyes close on a black bench in Brighton.

Canibus Idol

Outside a small record shop in Central London, it's a cold night a few months later, I am waiting to see my Idol Canibus. He is my favourite rapper. There's a small crowd of kids spitting rhymes to each other in circles in the alley waiting for him. When he turns up to perform everyone goes nuts including me. This guy's first biggest song is a diss track to another rapper LL Cool J one of the biggest rappers in the game. In his music video, he had Mike Tyson training him in a boxing ring in a temple, it was the best thing I'd ever seen. At talent shows, I would rap over his instrumentals and there he was, my Idol just a few feet away. I brought a mix tape along with me that I made at home using a cheap mixer, microphone and some software I cracked from the internet. I am hoping to give it to him.

After the show, he's chilling outside surrounded by fans. He's a short guy, slim no big bodyguards or anything. Trying to play it cool I stick my copy of his album in his face without saying a word, and he signs it. Just as he gives it back to me I slip him my mixtape. He says thanks then slips it in his pocket. My mixtape is in my Idols pocket. I hope he listens to it.

Later that night in my room looking at the CD my phone goes off. It's a text. It says "Canibus." I look at it for a minute like no way. I text back "Don't lie who this." Then I get another text saying "Can't you call the text number" Wait a minute, is Canibus telling me to call his phone. I'm bricking it. Nervous as hell it's like I'm about to ask out a super model. I ring the number. The ringing tone cutting the tension in the room. What if he doesn't answer? What if he does? The ringing stops. "Yo." I'd recognise that voice anywhere. It's him, Canibus on the other end of my phone. Still trying to be my coolest self I try to talk like a human being but I can't. He tells me my mixtape is illest. The illest rapper alive to me, my Idol, my inspiration, the guy who had a beef with Eminem is telling me my CD is ill. This was as good as it got.

He says we got to do a track together. I'm like err...sure. My Idol wants to do a track with me. No way. That's got to be any teenage rappers dream. He hangs up the phone. Wait, does this guy think I'm signed? I think he thinks I'm already with a label. What do I do now? How do I set up the track? Maybe he'll call back.

Days pass and he doesn't call. I'm too nervous to call him because I don't know what to do next. Weeks pass and eventually I text him, but there's no reply. He must have gone back to America. I never hear from him again. Idols in this world can't do anything for your life. Not really.

CHAPTER 3

Leave me I'll Die

I'm nineteen and my first love is a psychopath who studies psychology. On a double decker bus going passed Ealing around midnight, I'm on the way to see my currently suicidal girlfriend. On the other side of my mobile phone are tears of desperation. Light rain showers outside the windows of the bus only a few roads away from her house. Tapping the seat with my free hand, I can't get there soon enough but I don't want to go. Earlier that night I had tried to break up with her. So why was I rushing to here so desperately? She told me that she's in her car and if I leave her she's going to kill herself. I'm not sure what she's planning to do. Maybe she's going to drive into a wall. All I can hear down the phone is a mess of chaos and broken glass floating around her head. It's been two hours, the time it usually takes me to get to hers from where I live. I could have been at home in my bed

Running down the long and winding road, I can't help but feel as though I'm running into a trap. Earlier I had sprung free from the tyranny of her dictatorship. The obsessions, the jealousy the spiteful tongue, I couldn't take it anymore. Yet I'm running back to save the enemy of my heart, why can't I let her die? My life would be better without her and she'd probably be happier without me. Someone who is more of a doormat. Running toward her house from the bus I've stopped then seen a ghost run out of me. I've turned back. I've gone back home to sleep, it's a ghost that goes to rescue this psycho.

My ghost turns on to her road and sees lights on of small grey car. There's a silhouette of a shape in the seat. Standing till my ghost can feel no wind outside this suburban house. Upstairs pink curtains of her bedroom window flutter. Maybe her ghost was in the house. Walking over my ghost slowly opens the car door and there she is, tears running down her tan coloured face. Her streaks of blonde and brown a mess but my ghost was hers to keep. She messed his head up and confused him with her niceness until the dark side of her was forgotten in revealing clothes and cheap smiles. It wouldn't be long before the real her came back. Emotionally she traps my ghost whenever he tries to leave. Tears, sexy outfits, emotional blackmail. She tells him no one will ever love him like her. My ghost is chained in her black heart.

Chalk and Wine

Somewhere in south London, I'm in a cosy restaurant with my first no long after. A warm red light is cast on the walls from the hanging lanterns around us. I and the first girl I knew are eating out after I'd taken us here for a romantic meal. The love that blossomed between us was drunk with the wine that graced every table we sat by. The drink is something I never thought to order but for her, it was an expectation. As natural as breathing. She is short and tanned with a thick body. She's wearing a figure hugging dress with floral patterns exposing the shapes of her body and the skin of her legs. She was a feast for any eyes that laid own on her.

As the night covered the window in more night we dined on food that tasted as hollow as our conversation so we drank. Her glass is always more full than mine. I hate the taste of wine, but we had to keep to each other's level of drunkenness. Whoever is sober doesn't get the same jokes as someone who isn't because the levels of stupid wobble.

With not much to say, I bring up the conversation of something I'd heard recently. Suicides' mum was talking to us about her eating habits when she was pregnant. She told us that she ate chalk for calcium. It's an odd thing to recall, but I found it interesting so I told her. A dark red, a maroon covered her face like a spotlight showing a sudden vicious mood. Expecting something of a reply, a surprised comment or something along the lines of really, that's weird. Instead, she stiffens up. Goes quiet as I awkwardly sip from my glass. "So you're saying you would feed me chalk if I was pregnant," She said tapping her finger while the wine glass shook in-between her hand. I tell her I don't know, that maybe it might be good for you. Not that I knew or even cared it was just small talk. "So you're saying you would feed me poison to kill the baby," She said staring dead into my eyes. What the hell. The world became a frozen wasteland where all time and sense had been made still, unable to move freely through her drunken trance. Telling her it was just a story I heard makes her angrier. She actually thinks I am trying to make something up to poison her baby. By the way, I should mention she's not pregnant.

It's happened again. Every night that we shared even if it started with us being happy was doomed as soon as the wine came out. Each time she messaged me to bring a bottle, each time I ordered it, each time it ever came out of its cellar it tormented us like. At some point like an evil spell, it would transform her into a paranoid freak who wouldn't listen to sense. She would become this spiteful, insensitive monster whose face scrunched up and tongue lashed.

She tells me she wants to leave and we continue to argue into the street until we get to a nearby bus stop. Under the watchful street lights, I am going insane because of her insanity. The alcohol had got to me as well. The red liquid inside me, a passionate heat spilled from my every pore. All the rage boiling inside me I want to break her miserable pouting face. How can she sit there being mad when I should be mad? It's maddening.

Walking over to her my fist is clenched I want her to shatter, to dissolve into pieces and vanish. The cars whizz passed us unaware driving home to their families and night clubs. Pulling my arm back, I let go the sound of frustration from my throat and punch the bus stop glass as hard as I can. As much as I wanted to I could never punch a girl in the face. The strike sends cracks outward from my fist onto the glass, but it's shatter proof. The cracks spread like the web of a spider over my fist toward my wrist. Straight away I could feel something is wrong. My hand feels hot, it won't move. Something's broken.

A bus pulls up behind me as I fall to my knees holding my hand in agony. It lets out that jet of air sound as it lowers itself to the pavement. Casually walking onto the bus, she leaves me on the ground. The bus drives off while I'm holding my broken hand like a porcelain vase I'd just dropped on the concrete. This was my first love. It felt broken and drunk.

White Gold

The world begins with a shadow which I step out of into the stencilled lights of shop logos and lampposts of Ealing Broadway. The cars flash past me as the rain falls turning white as they fall through beams of headlights and brake lights. Where I came from I can't remember, I'm twenty heading home late at night wrapped in my dark hooded jumper. My stomach is as empty as my heart. Stalking the roads I'm on the lookout for something to take. My footsteps leave small ripples in the shallowest puddles along the cracked pavement. Turning away from the lights I walk down the longest road toward my dreary apartment opposite my University of West London. My university. I hated that place and I was in the first year. A year I would deal with alone and eventually drop out of like a skydive from a plane filled with burning coursework.

Turning onto the road, I walk passed a small boutique. This area is full of trendy shops selling overpriced cupcakes. Outside the white shop, the door angles inwards joined to a window sticking outwards making a corner. Inside this corner on the bottom are six bottles of milk. The four pint-sized ones you get from the supermarket. They must be meant for the morning which I'm close to. But it's not just milk, it's white gold against the white door. There is no food inside my fridge at home. There is no money in any of my pockets from my jeans to my coats. I haven't eaten properly in days. The rent at my student place is too high and I'm out here on my own with no work. I've had to borrow dishes from the Indian couple living upstairs. They cook rice and curry every damn day I smell it through my thin plaster walls. I'm thinking I can make some cereal with this at least. Or maybe just drink hot milk. Something's better than nothing. Without a second thought, I rip one bottle of the pack and carry on my journey home

It's been about three minutes down the road. The rain is hiding in the clouds of dark grey mist above and the road is quiet. In the three minutes, they say you can boil and egg. In three minutes you can read two pages of a book. In three minutes after taking the milk, I hear cars pull drive toward me engines roaring like lions nearing their antelope. Turning around, I see two police cars screeching to a halt, one behind me and one in front of me. The white and blue bonnets gleam off the street lights. The thought never occurred for me to run as I took in the scene as if I was watching a movie. Where are the bad guys? Could these two police cars be here for me? Standing still in my hoody holding the bottle of milk I look around the unfolding play as the car doors swing open like wings. Four police officers surround me. There are three men and one women in white shirts and black body armour. Their belts thick and full of bags and silver handcuffs. Their skin is the colour of milk and their hair dark straw. Oh no, white police and here I am, a black boy in my hoody. "Where did you get that milk?" Said the first policeman who was tall and broad. He had a cocky walk and stood right in front of me. "What milk?" I said holding it by my side. "Carry on being funny we'll put you in the nick mate." Said the woman officer creeping up toward me with her hand on her belt. She was short and unattractive. She looked like she would play rugby with the lads. Looking around at the four policemen they closed around me like a net. One of them is on their radio, random bursts of static and noise coming from the black box on his shoulder. He's given a description of me. Icy three or something? Apparently that boutique had CCTV cameras. I didn't get it, was the milk a trap to bait homeless people? Was the shop owned by someone in the Met? They must buy their lunch at this place. I stayed quiet. I knew that if I said anything they'd put me in for the night, they had nothing better to do. The officer took my milk, I'm not sure if he's going to return it to the door or is going to put it in an evidence locker. He takes out his pad from his jacket and writes me a fine for eighty pounds and sticks it in my hand. You could have made the argument that if I couldn't afford a quid for a bottle of milk eighty times that would be hard for me. The female police officer still has her hand on her belt, she is itching for something to do. I wouldn't give her the satisfaction. They turn around and get back into their white and blue cars. Such colours are reserved for purity, peace and hope.

Years earlier I would sit in my empty home as a blue moonlight comforted my crying mother because we had been burgled of our television while we were sleeping. The police never showed up till the next day, here it took them three minutes. Had I of known back then I would have reported my milk stolen.

As the white knights ride off into the midnight to save another diary product I stand shell-shocked at the amount of backup they needed for me. I didn't know what to be more upset about, the fact I had an eighty pound fine or that I still had nothing to eat that night.

As the wind tries to calm me down with a slight breeze I turn around to see a church behind me. It was carved into the night with stone and grey rocks. It was tall and horrifying yet I knew there was a presence from my time in Sunday school. Looking up at the building I say "What the fuck." As if they church could give me a response. I knew it was just bricked looming over me. There was no answer from them. I couldn't step passed the opening in the wall leading to the entrance. It was as if there was a barrier between me and the doors. Though they were surely locked anyway and anxiety draped me in something that would not allow me to go closer. Not then, and never in any church after that night. All I knew then was karma came for me quickly. Quicker than my friends. God didn't want me to steal anything. Not even when I was starving.

Bonfire Night

I'm twenty-six under a starless black mass on bonfire night with my second love waiting for fireworks. The air has become winter and the branches around us in the park look naked and shiver. There is a box in my coat pocket and inside there is a small diamond ring on a silver band. The sound of the fireworks rocket into the black but the sparks dazzle for a moment then fizzle out disappointingly. It's not what I had hoped for.

A quiet part of the woods nearby beckons me to it so I take the hand of this tall light skinned girl with brunette hair. In this moment, I should feel a warmth but all I feel is the winter despite my thick coat. Every step I take into the woods it is like a mafia movie where a guys about to be shot in the head and buried. The further in I go the more I want to run away from her smiling face. She already knows having felt the box in my pocket earlier on the train.

Ready to be executed I'm on my knees about to take the headshot. Pulling the box out of my pocket I can't think of anything romantic to say so I just open it and hand her a silver revolver with one bullet in it. She takes it from my hand, holds it firmly then points it at my face. Silence sweeps the forest and she says, "I do." She pulls the trigger and the bullet goes through my head blowing the back of my skull onto the dirt.

Laying on the soil blood runs out onto my forehead.

Looking up, there are no stars, just fireworks pretending to shine as brightly. The winter covers me like a blanket and I feel numb. This is what my second love feels like.

Valentine's bass

Orange rays of streetlights fill my large apartment window by the docks in Island gardens. It's valentine's in our second year together. A week earlier I had booked us a surprise trip for two. The television is off and it's dead silent except for the sounds of notifications pinging back and forth. Things haven't been smooth sailing lately. Our connection is on the last bar. Telling her that maybe were not that good together as we used to be perhaps is a mistake but I can't help but say what I feel when I think it. The intention is to get a response like "you're right, let's try harder" That's what I thought, but in real life people don't say the lines you write for them in your own head. Sometimes they go off script and leave you speechless. "You're right, sorry" is her actual response.
A small bass wave vibrates inside my chest. Ringing her number the woman who answers is a robotic voice explaining to me what I already know which his that her phone is off. She's switched me off like a light and left the room. I'm in the dark. Despite not feeling much love the feeling of being left and not being able to get through is a feeling of utter powerlessness. You have no control over the situation you weren't expecting. You're shot and you're bleeding out on the floor with no way to get up.
The bass goes through my chest over and over as I try in vain to get through to her. Why do I keep hoping? The waves get larger drowning my heart in wave after wave of bass. Walking around my room only, the orange street lights give me company. I fall to the corner finding comfort in the

walls being so close to me. The vibrations from the waves of bass shake tears out of me as I realise what's happening, the whole world is a quiet earthquake.
Words she said to me before are ghosts behind the shaking walls. They say "Promise me we'll never break up..." Dirty cups and glasses on my dresser edge. The words echo around me "…that we'll be together forever. No matter what we'll always work it out." The voice says. She made me promise these things. Despite all the promises she runs off to rave in a club with her same friend on valentines leaving me behind. Unable to get through to her phone. I can only assume she went to forget with vodka shots killing any thought of me sitting here in the dark.

CHAPTER 4

Night Terrors

A few months have passed since she left and each night I lay awake fearing another night terror. In my bed, the duvet is creeping out at the end of the sheet where I haven't buttoned it up properly. Staring at the window all I can do is grow in frustration as how useless my blinds are. They are rickety and thin. The grungy beige does nothing to stop the orange streetlight from brightening my room at night as if it's not hard enough for me to sleep already. At least, I pulled up that dreadful red carpet. My landlord has a thing for the red carpet and dirty colours. These are the trivial thoughts that keep me from the darkness. I really don't want to fall asleep, I am too anxious about what might happen if I do.

The first time it happened was the worst because I had no idea what was happening. It was as if I died and went to hell. But now I know how to escape. Deep breaths wake me from the greatest fear I'd ever known. That's what I do when I'm there. I've learnt to breathe and wait for the shadows to let go of me.

Each time I fall asleep I am not awake or sleeping but, somewhere in between. A never realm full of spirits and demons. It's there my greatest fears are realised. Looking up at my ceiling I can see where I've painted over the white. That's the corner it comes when I fall asleep.

Almost every night this week a different spirit has come to me. What they want from me I don't know but I grow tiresome of their terrifying visits.

In this realm I shout but nothing comes out and I can never move. Paralyzed from the neck it has me pinned down. There's nothing I can do to stop the terror or the panic attack that comes with it. What's worse is that it all happens in my room, so when I wake fully I am reminded of my worst nightmare. I had always wondered why in the movies when someone had a nightmare they woke up and sat up sweating and breathing. Now I know. These nightmares followed me home for years. Perhaps I brought them with me during the night, I must be more careful where I go.

Demons in Ibiza

Flashing lights break up the darkness hanging on the walls inside a grand palace on my birthday in Ibiza. I'm twenty-eight in a huge rave. The ceiling is so high it disappears into blackness. Beams shine down like Gods with flashlights searching for our souls. Sharp cold smoke jets through the dance floor from large cannons surrounding our bodies making silhouettes in the rising fog. Screams of joy can be heard as we're hit by the blast. A heavy thudding bass sends tremors from the floor upwards controlling our bodies to shake and contort until our hands reach up to the dark. Ahead of us on a vast empty black stage is a man in a box which covers the lower half of his body. His hands reach down on to two spinning plates. Angels with flowing hair have no eyes hidden behind black shades and bottles held aloft next to him. Connected by the beat, they nod their heads in sync commanded by the man in the box. He moves us all in this ocean using wave after wave of synthetic sound. As it elevates to climax I reach my hands toward it as if I could grab it only to see my hands pass through the lasers, empty. The beat rises and the sounds swell up like a rocket about to take off. As I look around the sea of hands are above the waves as if we were content to drown. The beat drops and the hands come down pumping and flailing into the air in all manner of different directions and ways. A few moments pass, and it happens again. The sounds rise, our hands go up, the climax is coming and then…The beat drops. Again and again, we rise, fall and repeat. There is no goal at the end of the drop, merely the beginning of another climax. We are trapped in a loop of our pleasure.

Crumpling up an empty plastic bag I give it back to my friend Buddha. A short but talkative skin headed guy from Sri Lanka. Our heads go back and we swallow. We float on the sea waiting for it to overcome us. "Can you feel anything?" Said my Buddha swaying with disappointment. I said no as I too sway with disappointment. Waves are rising for another climax again but this time, there is a loud bang. Glittering confetti rains down from above like paper rain. The clouds burst from the jets smothering the whole crowd like the crests of rushing ocean storm. A curtain behind the man in the box drops to the black stage floor revealing the most spectacular sight. On red carpeted stairs and roman looking columns, there is an orgy of scantly glad bodies in a mixture of pagan and roman outfits. Naked women and men with high heels, horns and goat hooves strut around the stage. Pansexual, bisexual, homosexual, I don't know what it is but its more than all three of those put together in a bowl. Beside me is a naked woman is high on a podium with large star covered breasts moving to the intoxicating rhythm. So many things happening at once my senses are on overload, I don't know where to look, but I have my phone out taking pictures and putting the souls inside my device like Pandora's Box.

All of a sudden I've been taken over. Everything I possess has been possessed. My mouth has a tongue that speaks only nonsense. I and my Buddha had been talking to two German tourists, but they disappear as we both lose control over our motor skills and talk utter crap.

My hands have broken a glow stick which I've bitten and started to eat it until I spit out the chemical taste.

"Buddha…I just ate this glow stick…I think I'm going to die." I said to him staring at the broken stick while he carries on dancing with his jaw going side to side. For the next few moments, I contemplate that I may die and I freak out.

Leaving my Buddha in the sea on some unknown quest I forget him. I forget all about our relationship and who he is. I forget where I am and who I am. All I know is I am driven by my lust to swim the sea in search for something…only I have no Idea what my desire wants. I end up going around the club trying to high five as many people as I can including what look like a lot of transsexuals.

After a few hours of swimming, I find Buddha. He's unhappy we parted. Really unhappy. He complains about losing the German tourists. He was sure he was on to a sure thing, as always. But we weren't. As soon as we swallowed we were destined to be a turn off to anyone not on our level. Our emotions are weighing us down as the music turns to a hollow thump as we leave. I've lost my wallet and it's my first night here. All my money is gone and the chemical pleasure is dragging me down into a dark place. The tide is lowering and the wave is fading away leaving me washed up on a rocky road outside the palace.

Trudging back down a rocky path to the villa I notice something about the rocks in the ground as I stop to spit up. Faces with evil hollow eyes and mouths surface in the rocks and stare at me. Walking behind Buddha whose shoulders slump we're disconnected. Now doesn't seem like the time to tell him I can see faces in the rocks so I keep it to myself. After the initial euphoria and happiness there now is a feeling of complete sadness as the sound of the beat from the palace echoes like a volcano erupting further and further in the distance.

As we reach the villa I refuse to go in. I've never felt so paranoid. There are pillars holding up a roof on the balcony made of hundreds stone and rocks. The faces of demons have followed me into them. I can see them moving. Believing the demons are going to collapse the roof, I quickly go inside. Waking up my other friend Buddha's little brother and my longest friend little Buddha and I tell him about the demons, that they're going to kill us if we stay here. My friends are both laughing at me as I try to save them from certain doom. Pulling them outside they sit down away from me while I fall into a cheap plastic chair overlooking a beautiful landscape. Looking up into the pale morning sky I can see a portal, a tunnel rushing ahead of me. It's as if there is a whirlwind of transparent butterflies flying in a circular motion toward an invisible moon. My friends are filming me on their camera phone and I hear them talking. The chemicals…I had swallowed three different ones, but I was only supposed to have taken one.

When I wake up I vow never to see the demons again. Never to journey to the palace of darkness and flickering lights. Never to be controlled by a man in a box. Never to give up my control, the control of my body, my mouth, my tongue, my hands, my feet, my mind, my heart or my soul.

CHAPTER 5

White Envelope

It's morning in my apartment in Island gardens not long after beauty had been here. I'm twenty-nine in the hallway I'm holding an envelope. I hate them. It's not my birthday three hundred and sixty-four days of the year so I know it's never a birthday card. It's a credit card bill or money demand. I had put myself through university for an unhelpful degree and I was in debt to my very neck.

Tearing it open I pull out the letter. It is an eviction notice. What else can I do other than stare blankly? My eyes going from the paper to the walls to the floor. The council are knocking down my block of flats to build new ones with more homes. The irony is not lost on me. I hadn't the money for a new flat I had been out of work since my degree. I hadn't spoken to my mum since she kicked me out of her house again five years ago. What could I do?

This was the moment I felt the more heartbreak. As if the very last pieces had fallen to the floor and I was already dead. I loved my flat. It had two bedrooms, my music studio. Two floors. I loved the bricks around me but just like that. With one letter it's all gone. No matter what it is, if it's a promise in this world it can be taken away from you in a single letter.

A Box of Pills

I'm in the doctor's office sitting opposite a middle-aged Indian lady with wavy brunette hair. Gangnam style was the song still ringing in my ears. It was the opposite end of the scale to what I was feeling. A big Korean with a smiling face having the time of his life while I wallowed in self-pity and abandonment. I haven't done the dance nor will I ever.

Handing me a sheet with questions on it the doctor asks me to say the numbers next to statements I feel match my state of mind. It's multiple choice number one being normal and number three being most abnormal. Through each question, I have to say the number. Each time my voice chokes a little. I can't get any volume. The further I go down the list the more I realise how ruined I am. Until I get to the statements "How often do you think about dying?" I say three, all the time and I can't hold back the tears. I am actually depressed. Sure I'd felt down lately but the confirmation just kills. I am one of them. Those people you hear about.

She gives me a prescription on a piece of paper and tells me to take these every day. The name of these pills is so long it just sounds like something medical. They always give these things long names like *oxisycotropincalism*. Why does everything medical have to have so many syllables? Is it so we don't ask what's that ingredients are? She suggests maybe I talk to a counsellor, but I'm not someone who tells strangers my problems.

Outside the doctors, I gather myself as the breeze feels cool against my cheeks where my tears have dried. The whole world is a pavement grey and every colour washed out and faded. Walking down Manchester road all the people I see are still. A place among the depressed sad and the lonely. I am one of them waiting to be released from the pressure of finding happiness. That spark to reignite an absent passion. If I was depressed before I knew I was, now that I know I am, I feel even worse. I wish she has just told me I was having a bad day.

Sitting on the edge of my bed as if it were a cliff looking down into a canyon of rocks split by a streaming river I hold the box of pills. They rattle as I shake them. Looking at them I feel as though I'm holding a beast, a poison something that I can't let out. I don't want this pill inside me changing me, altering my brains, overpowering my mind. Would I be myself? I have enough trouble as it is deciding on who I am without adding another personality to the mix.

If I open this box I might as well jump off the cliff because I won't be myself and how can I live in the world when all I am is a mix of drugs and chemicals. I can't rely on this box of pills to save my life. It's not a cure, it was given to me to get me out of the office. This box isn't the answer. I don't know what is, but this is but it's not for me. I open the box and empty the contents over the cliff letting the pills fall like hailstones. Goodbye to the person I never became.

House of lost souls

It's the morning before the bailiffs will come to throw me out a few months before I'm thirty and I'll be long gone before sunrise. Where I'm going begs an answer to which I have just a blank expression. Drained of emotion my lack of care submits only to the gravity that his my depressive state. Orange streetlights once again fill my flat with a lonely mist of colour.

Standing in the doorway of my box room I look at the empty space that was once the heart of my independent record label. I'd sold my whole studio in pieces for a few quid. Where was I going to take it? Ever seen a homeless person with a card box and a recording studio? I see ghosts of all the artists standing in the corner where the microphone used to be singing and rapping. Every time anyone came they had to come back again. It was if this place has power over them. I see myself. I hardly move from the large black studio chair as the sun rises and sets through the window. My body becoming skinnier and skinnier, weaker and drained. My skin full of blemishes dehydrated from forgetting to eat. Being too busy to eat no prayers to remind me to live properly.

There are ghosts of loose groupies, traces of alcohol and bottles on the window sill. Just behind me, a young Indian girl is crying. Bending down to her I ask her what's wrong trying to pull the hands from her face. She tells me that it is because she doesn't think she is pretty. She wants me to tell her she is attractive. To kiss her but my second love is downstairs. Bringing her to her feet I send her back out into the party outside while I stay in the studio. The memory of her fades into nothing.

Leaving the room I see the ghost of myself drunk on the stairs in the midst of an early morning, sausage's burning on the kitchen stove. Ghosts of me walk around this flat, either drunk, lonely or with someone else who is just as lonely as I was, I am. All of us here that came and went in this place were a history of emotions left behind.

In my bedroom, everything is out all over the place with one suitcase opened in the middle of my room. My whole life has to fit in here, it's just what I can carry. In this room ghosts of failed love and souls who weren't ready for it. I see myself being kissed on the cheek in my bed before being left over and over.

Along the wallpaper that I'd put up, ghosts of actors and actresses I cast to shoot my first short film. In this scene, a girl is taking cocaine at a party before being dared to give a girl a lap dance. In the corner by the ceiling, I see the demons of my night terrors. In the corner down by the window I see where I caved in when my second love left me.

I close the zip on my suitcase. There's nothing I can take except a few clothes and CD's of my albums I made. I leave the television and an old vintage film camera I'd used for a prop in a music video.

I leave behind all the ghosts and demons as they stand around me. Looking down at me as the zip makes its way around the case. Standing up, I carry my case and walk through the ghosts on either side of the hallway. Passed the ghosts or party guests having sex in my bathroom, passed the ghosts of an Indian girl teaching me how to read tarot cards, passed the drunken partying ghosts on the staircase. Down the steps to the landing, I look into the living room. I see two Australian ghosts, two girls spray painting their names on a wall of a room I found no use for other than to let people graffiti it before they left.

In the kitchen I pass and nudge the door open just a little, a ghost of a couple, my fiancé and I eating a romantic meal I cooked for us. Two fools who think there in love when it's burning away like the candles on the table.

Opening the front door I take one last look at the apartment and all the ghosts of my past selves and all the lonely dream filled people who've come. I brought them here time and time again. To this place of lost souls. Feeling as though I'm sad my soul somehow feels relief. I leave and close the door for the last time. Leaving all the demons and ghosts behind me.

Home from the Snow

I have nowhere to go yet I am rushing there anyway. Down the hills of Abbey wood on the coldest night of winter anywhere is better than the place you started breaking down. The wind at my back swirls around me brushing passed as if I am walking through a crowd of ghosts hurrying away from the night as I go deeper into it. Flocks of snowflakes glide and flutter down to nothing underneath my black trainers. Their entire life spent falling through a dark sky. Thoughts echo in my mind, how many times must I cry down these hills? This must be the last time I leave that house.

Ahead of me are the train station lights piercing holes in the blackness yet they are too weak to overcome it. Walking toward an unknown destination with no bag, no money, no job and no more friends sofas I am about to lose myself to the bleakness.

Tires screech to a halt behind me. A car door opens and my name reaches out to me. Stopping just in front of the barriers I took a deep breath. It's the voice of my mum. She's come for me as if there were no other way I'd go. Either I get in the car and go back to what I remember as hellish or go forward into oblivion. Why can't I go upwards?

Over five years ago I got fired from a job and when I came home we argued then she told me to leave. This time, I was gone for years. That's how my whole life has been. Never planning for the future because I can never be certain of the present. That at any minute the rug will be pulled from under me. All I can do now is return home. Which I did, but we argued about light switches and I stormed off down the hills to the train station where she followed me.

I and mum are a love that never really connected. But

fate had brought me back to her and there was nowhere else I could go. The car engine murmurs as the pleas from behind me tug at my broken heart strings. I go back home. Hoping to find a love there from her that I never had before. Hoping to gather myself and start again, from nothing. I had no hope.

PART II. AWAKING DAYLIGHT

CHAPTER 6

A Golden Forest

Six months later I am standing In the middle of a large shop floor of my new job. Lost in my thoughts, I see the Girl in black who works here out the corner of my eye. She is twenty, petite wearing a flowing black from her head to her the floor. Just her face shows like a star in a midnight sky. "What are you thinking about?" Says a Girl in black who has slowed down beside me carrying a bundle of colourful dresses. "Life," I said breaking out of my paused state. It is an honest answer and I saw no reason to go with my usual response of "oh nothing." For some reason, I want her to know. Adjusting her clothes holding them with both arms she looks surprised. "Really," said the Girl in black. There is a spec of silence, she's analysing me. "What about it," She says. There is an emptiness about life. It just doesn't add up and something's missing, but I can't put my finger on it. "Everything in this shop is made of something physical, but inside me, there's something that's not, my conscious mind isn't. So why is that?" I said to her. She asks me if I believe in God. Well, sort of.

As the days pass at work and we talk around the rails on the shop floor it's as if we are in our own world. Around us, the colourful clothes of rails transform into leaves of the same vibrant colours. The rails sprouting upwards widen into brown trunks shooting for the ceiling. They rise so tall they break through the ceiling and it shatters around us while we look on at the new sky. We're in a golden autumn forest. There's no more shop. The quaking floor is soil and fallen leaves. The trees branches cross and connect across the sky as if it has cracked, but nothing falls except the golden, red and rogue leaves raining softly around me and the Girl in black. Her cape flowing against the leaves.

We look at each other then she notices something by a nearby tree. A pair of bows and arrows. She walks over to them and picks up a golden set. Quickly following behind her I take the black set. "These are so cool," Said the Girl in black.

We walk together through the forest talking about philosophy and such. She asks me my thoughts on religion. There is an apple hanging off one of the trees. I take aim and I give her a paradox about god. "Can god make a rock so heavy He can't lift it?" Releasing the arrow, I strike the apple pinning it to the tree. I am sure she'll have no answer. The girl shrugs her shoulders and pulls back the arrow on her bow. There is a coolness about her. Letting go of the arrow it flies through the air darting and tunnel's its way through the falling leaves and split's my arrow in two. "It is not really a paradox because firstly, God by His nature does what He wills and what is in His nature. For example, I can't one day wake up and say I want to run as fast as a lion because my nature is not that of a lion, so the question doesn't arise for God to create a rock as such because he does what benefit His majesty. Secondly, the paradox attributes human attributes to God, make sense?" She smiles at me and carries on walking leaving me looking at my broken arrow and scratching my head. "Yeah, God seems like a bit of a diva if you ask me," I said looking at my broken arrow.

Our arrows fly through the forest, black and gold darting toward the same target just from two different angles. Even when she shoots first I try to split her arrow but I always end up missing. It's not even that she's telling me things about Islam, yet the voices in my head that have come up with unexplained answers are fading. With each shot, I feel I am becoming less stubborn and more open. Like I used to be before the dark closed in around me and shut me down in a bitter and hate-filled winter.

One day the Girl in black takes out a book from her satchel. It's not a Quran it's a thin book that she has brought for me. She tells me to read it and return to the forest to tell me what I think. In the blink of an eye, she is gone and I'm back in the shop floor holding this thin black book with a picture of a man on it. He is wearing red underpants. After reading this book, the path would be made clear for me.

Golden Tidal Wave

In the tranquillity of a dockside bench In Woolwich South East London would come to see a clear day after reading that book about Islam at thirty-one. It's the end of summer 2014 and a calm breeze from the currents of waves reach my suit trousers and jacket. The light feathers of the white clouds and the peacefulness of the emerald green trees paint my scenery. The tranquil topaz of the blue sky finishes the top of the painting, it is a beautiful clear day. All the colours were from the same pallet. Who could make pick such perfect colours and draw them across the same scenery? What colour would you have picked for the leaves through the seasons? It all seemed a picture to amazing. Each colour couldn't be without the other. No trees with no clouds. No clouds with no sky. It just clicked.

From underneath the great blue sky, I see a tall wave coming my way toward the dock. It's over a mile high and the crest as white as a thousand angels flying. The wave is not blue its golden shimmering like the suns reflection. It's not water, it's a tidal wave of a thousands and thousands of shining golden arrows falling from the sky. They fall around me killing my stubbornness, my confusion, my ego, my doubts, my anger, my bitterness and my past. All my pains from loves gone by shot dead on a green battlefield of roses and sharp blades of grass. There is one final arrow falling. It is as long as a spear. It searches through the sky toward me. I'm not afraid. I let it hit me right through the chest and into my heart. I have been struck by the greatest love there is and it came from God. Not a girl, not an apartment. It came from no one else but the creator of love itself and in that moment I'm dead but I'm alive. I believe in God and there is only one. His name is Allah (SWT). That's how I came to the Islam, by the docks on a clear day.

CHAPTER 7

A Mothers Love

When I tell my mum I'm Muslim, I'm going to be met with disapproval. Why do I know this? Because my mum watches television. Anybody the watches television will have the world as created in a screen and will accept information as presented in bows and ribbons made with the skin of innocent children. Mainstream media is vile.

I'm on a bus travelling home from somewhere I'd forgotten. My mind is fury with intent over telling of truths I just have to say to my mum. There is no better time, there is no perfect time, and there is no planned time. There is no time I capture on a watch where the hands meet and time stops enough for me to gather my breath. There is no time I can prepare long enough. There is no comfort only fear and what time is there for that? None. No, I am unafraid. Because I know time is neither on my side nor against me but is always now. So now I'm going to tell my mum that

I'm Muslim and she will know that the times are about to change.
Holding my phone closer to my face than usual I text mum that I need to speak to her later. Her reply is anxious as expected. She probably thinks I will tell her I got somebody pregnant or I'm going jail. I text her back saying don't worry it's nothing bad.

As I am on the bus about ten minutes later my phone goes off. Opening the text message icon I see mum has text back. She's angry, what have I done? The text reads something like "How can you, who do you think you are you can't install sky television in my house?" Some kind of random angry text like that saying I'm going to do something to her house without asking. I'm not angry, simply smiling and reply to her I don't know what you're on about, I don't even have a television? A few minutes pass and she text back again "Are you sure you're not I've got a text from you about installing sky?" Still bemused I'm just like YO! Chill out I haven't sent you any other text like that I see you in a bit.

Now I know my mum is very particular about her house. Don't think you can buy a lamp and put it in the kitchen somewhere without asking first. She tells me that she got a text from me, but now she can't find it and I never sent one. The text has disappeared from her phone. I am sure whatever sent it isn't human, but it convinced her it is me. It's made it easy for me to tell her my news now she's in a mood to listen, she can't possibly be angry twice.

Taking a seat by at the dinner table I tell my mum to sit with me, she refuses and keeps her distance behind the cooker. We have one of those fancy ones that're in the middle of the kitchen with a chimney thing hanging down on top of it which I usually hit my head on a few times a week. There is a nervous anxiousness written across her face which is in her hands. I am all calm and smiley getting ready to tell her and she's impatient "what is it, what is it hurry up tell me." My mum says. Now I'm taking my sweet time because where do I start? With I am Muslim? Or do I work my way in? I go for working my way in. I start off with a little speech about life and she is not having any of it "Oh no you're not moving out are you, how can you be so ungrateful." Mum says interrupting me. "No, it's not that" I replied. Seeing that she's going to need the direct approach I just come out with it "Mum, I believe in God and I am Muslim now." I say to which I'm greeted with the most unimpressed face ever in the history of mankind. Most of my life I've been met with those faces of exhaustion, disappointment, frustration and anger, but this is the icing on the cake. My words are met with groans and "you're not going to be one of those extremists are you." Mum says with her face in wrinkles and creases. For the love of Allah I really hate television. "No mum, I'm not a terrorist," I say eyes rolling. My mum is taking it all in and doesn't really know what to say. I can tell that she's just worried, all the possible bad things she's heard about Islam rattling away in her brain.

My mum is a firm believer in money and bricks. Her second question is "You're not going to be wearing one of those dress things are you." Making a flowing gesture with her hands. She's talking about the thobes to which I reply "Maybe, but that's not even anything to do with practicing Islam, that's just clothes." She doesn't ask me any questions relating to Allah, why I believe in him or what my thoughts are. I try to explain that I believe in god and heaven but as I'm doing so realise I'm being stared at by someone who thinks I'm completely crazy. There, as she leaves for her room is me. In the kitchen with the lights dim. Disappointed she won't share in my happiness. But it's okay because the room is not completely empty. I have Allah now. I'm not alone anymore.

My name is Zakariya

A few days earlier before telling my mum about Islam. I'm in my bedroom and there are several yellow sticky notes on my desk. Each of them has a name written roughly across it. There Arabic Muslim names. The feeling has overtaken me to rid myself of my former self and chose and a new name for my future. Having asked for name suggestions from people, namely Girl in black she tells me the names she likes, one of them is Zakariya. At first, I'm like urgh. I don't like that name. I hate it. So each day by this desk I make D'ua to Allah asking him Oh Allah choose the best name for me.

So each day it's as if I am back in the golden forest. In front of me is a skinny tree with golden leaves. Each leaf has a name on it written in the pattern of the leaves veins. Each day I come here a sit by this tree and wait for the leaves to fall. Each name falls gracefully to the ground dying into a brown by the time it graces the soil. Every day I make D'ua and the names continue to fall. I don't like that one, I don't like this one. Until one day I come back to the tree and there is just one single leaf left hanging by a branch nearest to me. I mouth the name and all of a sudden it feels as if it's made for me.

Pulling it off the branch I pull it off the desk. I'm sitting in my room holding a yellow sticky note with the name Zakariya. I go to the mirror and puff out my chest and say my name again like yeah, Zakariya sounds like he'd be a good Muslim man. Just like that, I had my name. Settled. It stuck to me like glue. Didn't take me a second to get used to responding to it.
It isn't until after that I looked up the meaning of the mane.

That it meant remembers god. I couldn't have asked for a better meaning. That's the whole point of everything. Then, I read the story of the prophet with the same name. And, again it couldn't have been more of a match. Here is me, without anything I truly wanted. No wife, no home of my own, no kids and dying for an Islamic-inspired career. But Zakariya the prophet may Allah be pleased with him, he had to wait until he is ninety before the Allah blessed his barren wife with a child after he made D'ua. I'm thinking I got years on him. I can have patience just like him.

It is the perfect name for me. Even though most people have straight away taken to calling me, Zak. So now I'm Zak. But I don't mind because I love my new name. They guys at work help me change it by signing my deed poll documents. It only cost me twenty quid to get them online and the brothers and sisters were happy to sign them as my witnesses.

Friends with Buddha

Little Buddha, I call him my brother. He is about five foot, Sri Lankan and has a Buddhist background which is not hard to see. While he is not a follower per say he is very much into healing and is a spiritual person in that sense. A professional masseuse and yoga enthusiast there is a heart of gold in his chest. One of the most considerate people I know. He's also a social butterfly if that butterfly was on speed. His life as a Dj is chaotic and it's him I was visiting in Ibiza.

Where in a bar with brown varnished tables and a patterned carpet. We have soft drinks on the table after I told him I'm drinking orange juice. I tell him I am Muslim. At first, he's shocked. The look on his face is "WFT" How do you tell someone who doesn't believe in a god that you do? He's also a good DJ, he loves music with what he describes as "soul". So I tell him "you like music with soul, what is a soul?" I said. He says, "it's like an essence inside you." Looking into the air. I say "essence? Yea your soul" I replied. It goes back and forth like this for the next ten minutes. It's funny how everyone knows the word soul, and describes things as good when they have it but then not attribute it to anything.

He says I don't need a religion to tell me what to do. And there it is. That's the same S I used to say come to hit me in the face Argh! The problem is with this world people think religion is there to control you and tell you what to think. Read a Quran, then watch one advert on television. Which has devised a plan to get you to buy something you didn't need until you saw it and which has devised a plan for the entire universe? He loves house music, the last three songs I hear are Rumours a song where the lyric was "I am not looking for anything serious just something casual." Another is can't stop where the lyrics are "this music makes me high, I can't stop playing this song over and over, I don't want to get off this ride!" If music is your teacher you're going to fail the test of life I guarantee it. Try telling that to someone who says "Music is my life"?

My friend is convinced religion is control, and that we can do everything in moderation. I say to him, what is moderation? Some girls think a knee high skirt is moderation others think to step out in a see-through nighty and high heels are moderation. Some people think one glass of wine is moderation, others two. Who decides what moderation is then who moderates the moderators? Everything I say he's looking for a reply. Not that he's trying to take it in or consider it, he just wants to win the point. I'm not trying to be right just say what is. It is frustrating at first, but now it's kind of fun debating with him. It makes me think of more angles to give dawah. He's now a training simulator for dawah and all the things people will say back to you. All in all, he tells me "no matter what, what people say or anything that I got your back." He would eventually become more open and accepting.

As with all my friends oceans has come between us through no one's fault. I don't hang around with anyone from my past. We have different purposes and must follow where our hearts lead. For those whose hearts are black like mine was you'll find yourself in darkness depressed and unfulfilled by all your daily accomplishments. For those whose hearts let the light in even a little, you will find more happiness and satisfaction in the comfort of daylight and good purposes. I haven't a lot of friends anymore. But I'm an only child and I was built for isolation and I am grateful for the few friends Muslim and non-Muslims that I have now.

Rain on the lake

A sister finds me at work after hearing the good news. She is beaming with a sincere joy. "Welcome aboard the good ship Jannah," She says before remembering to add "Insha'Allah" She has been looking for me as she is leaving for a new job and hasn't had a chance to see me. Her whole aura is bright and it makes me feel as though I have joined something. Like I've been given a golden ticket to this secret ship about to launch toward the heavens. Well, she insists I took her Qur'an translation. Now, I don't know if this is a Muslim thing or a Bengali thing but when they offer you something you better just took it. You can't say no. Seriously, just accept it, smile and be gracious.

When I tell one of the other managers at work he tells me not to read it. That I won't understand it and I should only go through it with an imam. I'm thinking there's something wrong with that statement as I continue on my way.

Later In my room, the sun is peeking through my window nets. I' m reading and I get into it and it's just intense. Strong and powerful voices as one voice coming down from the clouds into me. It's like nothing I've read before. It's not from here. Something is opening inside me.

A veil is lifted from around me and flies across a desert terrain with smooth mountainous rocks and hills. Years of sweeping wind has made thousands of lines in them. Stripes of layers oranges, reds peaches and dusk. The sky is a solid and perfect baby blue. There is an impulse in me to follow the flowing silk of the black and gold veil shining from golden stitches.

The veil leads me to a small lake. It's made of a flowing crystal. Looking onto it I can only see the gleaming surface and a reflection of myself with a bemused yet fascinated expression. There are no ripples or trails following my fingers as I wade them in the cool water. A pearl falls onto the lake in front of me breaking the surface like a soft bullet hole. It's a raindrop. Looking more closely it's a letter. Slowly it sinks underneath. Then another letter and another. They start forming words and sentences hitting the surface then sinking. I'm reading a verse, a verse from the sky. Reading as fast as I can, there are sentences causing me ore. There are words and pictures being drawn with rain on the lake. Some I can see, some familiar while others wash my brain with an unimaginable honesty. But there are some words of rain sinking too quick for me to grasp. Some ayahs, some surah's sinking before I can understand them. One ayah is written across the lake but falls before I get it. "Wait…what" I say to the sky. Before I've grasped it another ayah across to my left appears and vanishes.

There is only one thing I can do before this ayah is lost. Standing to my feet as I'm soaked in the words of God

I know I must dive in deeper. That I have to concentrate to get in this lake and understand that verse.

"Stop, don't go in," Says a voice from behind me. Turning around, I see a figure of a man on a rock wearing a long maroon tattered cape and a tall hood covering half his face in shadow. The sky is now grey from the gathering of all the clouds and the rain pours heavy. "You shouldn't go in there." Says the man. Clenching my fist and frowning I ask him "Why not?" Looking around, he hesitates "It's not safe for you in there, you might drown." He says. Looking back on the lake I don't know who this guy really is but I can see the words falling into the lake and I can't wait. If I drown then let it be. Let me drown knowing what I didn't and let me die believing in what I couldn't before.
With a deep breathe I dive into the lake after the surah. Into the lake the pearls of wisdom shooting past me as if they were fired from a sniper's bullet into the blue all around me, but I have no fear. I'm searching for the surah. As I open my eyes and the bubbles clear oh my god the lake is a vast ocean. The seabed is endless and the edges are blurred with blue. The pearls twinkle in this sea like starts in an infinite galaxy. Where am I? This deepness is further than it looked from the surface. There are bright rainbow colour coral reefs with creatures made out of clear glass flying around me.

I see the surah sinking to the ground in broken pearls floating. Reaching my hand out, I grab some of the pearls and clench my fist around them. Just a couple words. My breath I running out. I don't think I can capture all these pearls at once. It's too much to do in one dive. Rising to the surface as my face breaks the waves.

I'm back in my room. Each time I read the Qur'an over the next few weeks I dive in, again and again, catching new pearls and take them with me. Some I forget at the lake. Some surah's I still can't grasp or are too deep for me, but I know it's only a matter of time until I can reach new depths. But it's infinite. I know it will take time. The man in the hood never showed up again.

CHAPTER 8

Dreams of love

You never know how you end up in a dream, no beginning no end just an abstract middle. Sort like how life is, you don't remember the very beginning or will you the end. It's all one big confusing abstract middle. Tonight I wake up in one of three dreams that would change my life.

In my first dream and I'm in the middle somewhere in a cave but it has no walls it's just pure black all around me. In the near distance is a beam of light, a single beam of wide light coming down piercing the darkness. I can't see where the light is coming from, but it's from high above me. The shower of white surrounds this girl. It's Girl in black. Showered In the same black from head to toe as the black. Just her face and hands showing. I see her eyes looking at me but as I take a step forward her eyes roll up to the top of her head and she's looking up into the light. It freaks me out. I step back and she looks at me again. Okay, so I step forward and her eyes leave and go up toward the light again.

I know she only has eyes for god that she likes me, but she loves god already. I know I can't treat her like the others. It's a dream I'll never forget, and would be the first of three.

The Second Dream

Journeys home are always the best. Nothing beats the feeling of coming home. The place where you feel warm and secure, and you know you can just go in throw off all your clothes in a pile and watch movies. I fall asleep another night and I have another warm dream.

I open my eyes and I'm laying down facing up at Girl in black. We're in the backseat of a black car with black leather interior. She is cradling me with a warm smile. A nurturing motherly smile, I actually feel like her own. Her own child, secure and tranquil as she looks down adorned with her glowing black scarf and cape. Outside the back of the car window it's raining, but not like a storm but still heavy. Though it's peaceful as the car rocks gently. With her, I feel as though I am on the journey home.

The Third Dream

When you are in a place where beauty is your view from all sides you know you're in a beautiful place. You feel safe there and peaceful as you look over trees and greenery. It's somewhere the lights of the city can't reach you. A forest is a place of peace and what better way to realise your inner self.

In my third dream, I am in a beautiful and tranquil forest. I have that same sense of peace I had in my other two dreams. It's like I've been here before. Maybe as a wandering soul through these dream worlds. Here, a big massive tree with a thick trunk is ahead of me. It's a glorious tree, but it's still humble looking not over flourishing just a roof of branches giving shelter over a little clear area. Around it is a few people, not many. I can't see their faces because there on the edges of my sight. But I'm not afraid of them.

I am by the tree and there are two people, one is an imam and the other is Girl in black. We're getting married. Joined In the beginnings of dawn in a clear forest with just a few shadows watching. I feel as though this is the most pleasant feeling of peace. It's pure, free from the chaos of normal dreams. It's calm and slow and it feels as though I was always meant to come here, always meant to discover this place where she is already waiting.

I trusted that Allah had sent her to me and I trust Him completely. I knew then I had to marry the girl in black and I would tell her the very next day.

B L A C K

In my room, I wake up and the walls are far and wider than usual. The ceiling higher and the light escaping my curtains net brighter. My first thought is to tell the Girl in black my dreams and in doing so that will be my proposal to her. My heart is beating stronger than usual, but I'm not afraid. What time is there to be afraid anymore I've been through all the heartbreak I can possibly go through? I've been at the darkest places I could possibly know. I am a man who has nothing to lose.

A few hours have passed since I've sent her my dreams online. I see a notification. She's responded. The letters beneath the glass press against the screen and filter into my heart. At first, she is surprised. I see letters O M G and W O W. I guess you would be but as I read I can tell she is feeling a mix of emotions even by her sentences. There is a feeling of yes and no in everything she says. As the letters keep filtering into my room through the screen they illuminate around me. I see letters S U R E and I tell her that I am she says, but it could just be a dream. I tell her I know it isn't. I know the dream didn't come from me. A dream that pleasant could only come from somewhere else. Besides, this is how it works. I've found in you a righteous, content, passionate and intellectual mind wrapped in soft beauty. What is there not to be sure of?

She tells me she is happy that I would consider her as a W I F E and not a girlfriend. I had no time for girlfriends. Not anymore. As I'm buzzing the paragraphs become longer. There is a problem. It would be hard for her to bring a boy to her P A R E N TS. I wonder why as my eyes follow the sentence. She says they would think we'd been dating, up to all sorts. Frowning I brush this off in my head as a minor thing. You could just tell them the truth. That we met at work, we talked and I proposed. Simple. Or so I thought. The paragraph keeps getting longer the letters filling my room which had suddenly become a lot smaller. It is a small box around me.

She says that because she is the E L D E S T daughter and there's some kind of example she has to set to her sisters. I'm following the words, but I don't see how she wouldn't be setting a good example. Then as I watch the words continue I follow a sentence that spills letters from A to Z but most notably stopping on the letters B L A C K. There is a problem because I am black and she is from B A N G L A D E S H. I can see, I can feel the letters S H A M E. I can see C A N'T and W O N'T.

The letters on tragic letters filter through my screen surround my light bulb and cover it until there is no more light. My room is black except for a small pin holes light between the inks. I type back sending my own letters. I'm M U S L I M. I thought I'd left racism and discrimination behind me. In that other world. The world without light, how am I greeted with darkness once again? I thought we were all the S A M E now. I thought I had a valid passport how is there a border I can't cross.

Her parents won't A G R E E. She isn't allowed to marry who she wants. They would prefer a non-practicing Bengali over me. There is a shame over my colour in her community in east London and Whitechapel. But they don't realise, the shame has already been laid over them as tightly as their own scarves. I have nothing to be ashamed of in my pursuit of the other half of my H E A R T.

The Black Kite

I'm in my box again, at home during the day fading into the night like water colours mixing on a canvas outside my window. We've been messaging, the Girl and black and I. We have come to place where we are unsure of where we stand on a rocky surface spreading beyond our sight to an unclear horizon. What do we do now that we want to be together but cannot be sure?

In my past if I wanted someone I would just go to them. But now, I have to wait over the ignorance of closed hearts in a house I'm not invited to in an unknown place.

Among the pale blue sky and oak, the brown desert floor of this unknown place a woman in a pink dress flies a black kite. The kite wishes to be in the white cotton of the sky but is held back the by the long rope it's attached to. The kite struggles and writhes in the air to free itself. It begs for freedom, but it can't shake its leash. The kite knows there are higher levels of this world it wants to explore under Gods sunlight. The black kite dreams of walking on carpets of clouds. The winds batter the silk fabric of the kite teasing it, asking it to join them swirling in the air, but the kite can only go so high. Held down from beneath by the fear of letting go.

My voice is caught by a gust of wind and carried off far away from the woman in pink as I try to tell her to let go of the kite. Walking toward her body, I get closer with intentions to take her hand from the thin rope. Her dress is decorated with gold sequences and thread reflecting the day. Her face is a mystery, but I unravel it in my mind as I draw nearer. Calling to her she does not turn around. The kite waves and swims above us. I stop just a breath short from her shadow.

"Let go of the kite," I whisper softly as not to startle her. She holds on to it firmly. "Let go of the kite," I whisper again. I know she can hear me because the wind has let my words be carried passed her falling on the brown soil on the other side of her contempt. Perhaps she will never let go.

Reaching into her shadow, I grab the rope and break it setting the kite free into the blue sky. The woman falls to her knees and cries into her hands tears watering the earth. No grass grows where she cries. Looking above the sun shines through the edges of the clouds blessing the kite with a silhouette as it finally flies free.

The thought to grab the rope occurs to me, but this kite is not one to just be passed from one hand to another. Placing a soft palm on the woman's shoulder I look up and watch the black kite fly for the first time. Higher and higher reflecting in the glass of our eyes.

Back in my bedroom. My box. The black kite is firmly grounded. We ask each other what to do. We decide that it's best to stop talking. To part ways so we don't become attached. What if we do and there is heartbreak for us when they don't allow us to fly? So we decide to make Du'a and pray for what we want. But we won't speak again at work, or online. Our sky remains worlds apart.

The Grey Mountain

Walking through the shop floor reminds me of the forest where we could only go in my mind. My coat is long and thick from the weather covering my slender frame. Keeping me to myself. The lights beam down on my from a black ceiling above that fades into nothing around the spheres of light. Around me, ghosts buzz from dress to cardigan to the latest trend. There is hardly any room to move, nor a straight line to walk to avoid their unconscious gazes. There are all a blur to me. Faceless women and lost children hiding in among the rails with innocent smiles.

Opening the door to the stairway I'm confronted by the dreariest of greys on the walls. To my left the grey ascending steps. The door shuts behind me as I climb the first slope of the grey mountain. My head is low over the first few rocks then I hear light taps of feet coming toward me. Lifting my head up there is a washed white sky overhead stretching out with clouds stitched together bound by their sadness about to cry rain. Down the mountain of jagged grey steps with black shades, I see a flying black cape fleeing from the back of a petite silhouette just coming into life through a flowing mist of cloud. It's the Girl in Black.

My lips widened and my jaw falls to let out the trapped words in my heart. But before I can speak she has looked at me. In my eyes but only as the second split in half. Her eyes ran from my own to the mountain floor avoiding contact. She took a breath as if she had seen me as a wanted murderer. Life flushed from her face and she walked passed me without a word, her black cape flowing sailing by in silence. As she faded from sight my head did not turn to follow her she was already gone. There I am at the beginnings of the mountain standing still like a statue made of rock. What I'm doing is taking in the scene around me feeling that I'm the only man on the mountain. I know she wanted to smile, I know she wanted to say a salaam. But she tried her best to suppress her love for what is right. But yet everything in the way she passed me felt wrong. I carry on up the mountain alone to the top. I clock in at the machine and look forward to hours and hours of work without her voice.

Our Cinema

The movie has begun and you have walked in to see the Girl in black and me across the big screen in the cinema. You are there with your secret love in the only place you can be alone. Where no one can see you hold hands, where no one can see you kiss. On the big screen, my restricted love is being played out over laptops and phones.

The last scene we tried to distance ourselves, but the silence never lasts. Our smiles to strong our souls to familiar. Our hearts already joining, stitching themselves together with golden thread. This is despite our attempts to walk the other way on the straight path. If two people who have the desire to be together walk another way from each other long enough they will meet half way around the earth. As the Prophet (SAW) said for those who love each other nothing has proven as good for them as marriage. *Sunan ibn Majah.* (Hadith) But the community will not see.

I've wanted to take her to the cinema, but she won't entertain the idea. Instead, I message her online asking her what film she wants to watch. I send her a link then I tell her when I press play. I am always slightly behind. In our homes in what seems a million miles away, I watch a movie with her. We message each other through the film. Who we think is the bad guy. She makes up the names of characters and we try to figure out the twists. Whenever a black guy comes on screen I tell her that's me. I can't wait to show her my favourite Will smith and Denzel Washington movies. We laugh, we skip the sex scenes and the swearing together. I didn't realise how much bad language and sex there was in films. If I see it I tell her to skip. She messages me that she's closed her lid. Not her eyelids, her laptop.

This is as close to her as I can get. Letters on my screen making pictures of her face. People may judge, tell me it's wrong because that's easy to do. But what do they do? I know my heart's intentions and limitations, this is the least I can take. In over a year to not have touched her, seen her hair, or shared the smallest kiss is the best I can do. I can give up a lot, but I won't give up movie nights.

CHAPTER 9

The White Plan

I've got to come up with a way to marry this girl. I can't just sit here and do nothing so I make a plan. The Girl in black is with me on the shop floor and I break it down to her ocean's eleven style. I'm going to invade East London Mosque, the girl's dads local. He respects the Imam there. I'm going make friends and get him to convince the dad to let her marry me.

Step one, I go to Zara and buy all white clothes I need to be noticed. Make sure I go to the mosque and get front row so everybody sees me. I'm a six feet tall black guy so that will work. Step two, make sure to salaam all the uncles. Mostly they'll mumble but the odd one lights up says salaam and gives me a perfume to rub on my hands. Step three, take a few sickies off work so I can go to the revert circle in the mosque on Saturday, I hear the Imam comes there sometimes to speak to the reverts. Step four, I make sure I come across as the nicest person ever and ask him loads of questions so he knows my character is good. Step five, get him to go to the Girl in black's parents and convince them to stop being racist and be the good people they are and let me come to the house to meet. Step six, I ask the Girl in black about her dad mum as favourite things, what do they like? Step seven. I buy a new suit, and make sure I'm dapper because I hear that Bengali parents prefer guys in suits rather than thobes. Step eight, I get all the brothers of work to sign a sheet of paper, tell them it's for a petition to get me married and to show all the brothers that think I have good character. Should get at least a dozen signatures. Step nine. Turn up at the house with a basket of all the family favourite things and the petition and a speech. Step ten, eat her mum's biryani and say it's the best ever and don't let them know the spices are too hot. Drink plenty of water. Ask the dad to give me advice on life then, make a speech. Probably steal something, a mixture of Martin Luther king, Mufti Menk and Tupac. This will make them crumble into tears and they'll say I can marry her daughter. Perfect.

So, I am in Zara at Westfield for step one and I buy all the clothes. Something contemporary, not a thobe but still white so I stand out. I get white trousers, t-shirt and a white jacket. On to step two. I go to the mosque and I met my mentor from there Abdullah and we listen to a talk. Oh, wait. The talk is about sincerity. The Sheikh is talking about people who come to the mosque with intentions other than to worship Allah. He talks about coming to the masjid just to meet someone who they might do a business deal with. Talking about people who come to the mosque for themselves with a secret motive rather than Allah. Seriously, I am sitting there thinking I've come all this way from South East London to this mosque to infiltrate it and this is the first talk I sit in.

This is what makes me know Allah loves me when he stops my plan at stage two. I didn't want to take a chance and be the guy the Sheikh was talking about. The truth was I came to the mosque for her and not for god. God had me figured out. I couldn't go through the plan. I couldn't use the masjid or the Imam for my own means. I had to do what I did for God. Really and sincerely. That meant going to my pray at my local. And praying for her from far away

Waiting at the gates

In a small cubicle in the changing room mats stacked in a corner. A crudely hung prayer time table is in the opposite wall. It's time to pray and I've managed to pull myself away from the stress of work and the busy people. Locked away, I am ready for peace where the sunlight cannot reach.

Taking a deep breath I make my intention (niya) and I say to the wall "Allahu Akbar" Allah is greater and at that moment, the walls break and crumble around me as if they were each attached to a rope from the outside pulled by a giant. The bricks, the walls the grey neutral and dull walls thrown into the air in slowness revealing a majesty of green fields and trickling rivers.

There in the middle of the green, I stand with my shadow at my side arms crossed. He wobbles back and forth and I give him a look so he knows to stand straight. I used to pray with my eyes closed, but now I know better and I can see the beauty of Salah. It is a field spanning across several horizons beyond rolling hills. Here I can see hundreds of other Muslims in their white cloth praying towards the same direction shadows cast beside them on to the solid pure green grass. At any prayer time, hundreds and thousands of us all come to this place. All manner of butterflies and silent bees hovering around rainbows of flower bushes.

Beyond the direction of our prayer lies a glorious gate.

Magnificently built toward the clouds outlined by rays of uplifting light. Through the iron gates, huge domes of pearls sit among the field as a city forming a constant skyline of minarets. Here in prayer, we are in front of the gate of paradises. With each Salah, we open our eyes just that little bit closer to the gates of heaven. Deep breaths, every prayer is in slow deep breaths trying to keep me from racing through this moment. By my feet slithers of water that look like worms speed passed and over my feet washing away the minor sins.

There is the song playing in my head, all of sudden I see a rapper dancing on top of a Rolls Royce. The scenery around him cracks and falls to the floor revealing more and more of this random music video. It's that stupid song everybody's been singing stuck in my head. Making me lose concentration. Focus. Praying louder in my head I manage to make the pieces of heaven float back into place covering up the rapper making him and his hoes disappear. Where was I? What rakat am I on? I think it's the second one. Let me just see how I feel, if it feels right to stay and do Tasahood I'll do it. It feels okay. No doubts. I am at peace again. Looking beyond the gate. That is where I want to be and this is the way toward it. The stress of work is leaving me as perceptive of the trees huge in stature make my problems feel so small.

Beginning to end the prayer I flick my finger out. Still not sure if and when I am doing it is right I just do it anyway. It's something I'll have to figure out. Reciting the finishing part of the prayer the air… "Fucking car park bruv," Says a voice from beside me. To my left, the scenery has split and there is a large hole into my workplace cubicle. Two brothers I know are outside the cubicle. I recognise their voices. "Fuck, breaks only fifteen minutes though how you gonna fucking…get back in time." Says another voice in reply. Trying to focus on the gate I take a deep breath and try to recite my Darood. "I was completely broken out of my place and I rush to finish the last prayer with all the swearing outside. I say my salaams and just like that I'm back in the cubicle. Back in the grey.

I can go outside and tell those brothers what for, but they didn't know I was in here. So I stay until they leave as not to embarrass them.

The Deadline

My bedroom walls are painted a washed yellow sunlight. At the screen again inside my box, I'm thirty-two and it's been a year since I told the Girl in black I wanted to marry her. We've been back and forth through periods of waiting. The Girl in black says her mum feels Reverts should marry other reverts. I'm an outcast. Not quite as good as the "Born Muslims." I haven't practiced Islam my whole life but how Muslims have? She has tried to converse on the issue with her parents, but they are stubborn. It will be a case of who is more stubborn. I think who is in the right should be firmer.

In six months, when April comes and she has finished university if by this time there isn't an accepted proposal, if her parents don't even agree to meet me then we will move on. That is what we have agreed to do even if I don't really believe what we're saying. I feel like I'm lying to my heart.

It's a deadline, six months from now our lives are going to be saved or the plug is going to be pulled. Side by side in hospital rooms we lay unconscious in comas unable to break free from the state of ignorance that surrounds us in Whitechapel hospital. We crashed into each other at a speed when she came out of nowhere. I didn't even see her until she had hit me. Then I was gone. I blacked out and all I could see was that colour. That colour wrapped around my sight except for a face. A fair skinned face full of sweetness and light that stayed with me in my coma. Six months from now in April when we have dreamed as much as we can we will awake together or the plug will be pulled and we will drift into the unknown. Each of us alone. Only God knows if we will survive the crash.

Whatever happens, if doesn't work out, if she changes her mind Alhamdulillah Allah wrote it this way. I will play my part and accept the next chapter all the way to the end. The best things come from the darkest places.

It's December 2015 now. April 2016. The deadline.

Fade to Black

UNSTRUCTURED POEMS

Poem:
A thin sheet of glass

I carry a love not on my arm and not in my hand. But everywhere I go it is with me. Her body is covered by sheets of glass. Her Body is covered by black words and letters wrapping around her behind a glass screen. The touch screen is close to a touch. My finger moves across the glass caressing her face. Her skin is a mystery to me only the future knows. Only the future could tell me how soft it is and how long her hair is. Only the future can tell me how warm her breath is on my neck while she sleeps. Only the future can tell me what her heart beat sounds like In the dead of night or the wake of the morning. Between the touch of our hands is glass. From each side we send letters to each other in love so are they love letters? We stay up and we fall asleep tighter from other sides of the city. Only the future knows if the glass will break.

Poem:
Keeping us in the fire

Allah says we will all taste fire and if it weren't for his mercy we'd all be hell bound yet they, the deniers would keep us in the fire because our colours are from separate paints. They, the deniers will keep us in the sins they judge us for, they will keep us burning so they can please themselves. They, the deniers will say we should not be committing Zina yet they will keep us where we have to hide. Saying we must be halal yet they make what we do Haraam. They, the deniers will say it's wrong but deny us from doing right. They, the deniers with their opinions will keep us in the fire falling deeper into a love they say is forbidden then they will cry, why did you do this? Some may say sorry, but I won't. I will never apologize because when I came to marry your daughter you would not even see my black face. So I kept my face in the darkness around the flickering fires, waiting patiently for your daughter until I could wait no more. And for all the sins they say we made they must look down on their own hands and see them burnt. They, the deniers were the ones who kept us in the fire.

Poem:
Feeling human

I don't know what it is, I don't want to put her up on a pedestal. But I have to admit there is something different about her. There is a peacefulness around the body like a calm breeze whispering around a slender tree. I feel lifted. Supported and encouraged to be better. Do to better. For her, for me, for my lord, for the world. I haven't felt human for so long I don't know how to react.
I'm just calculating all these moments we share. Processing, understanding why I'm laughing I didn't expect to. She must be funny? Trying to put these interactions into perspective I keep coming back to the equation, she's good for me.
Something is so sincere about her, they're no lies in her, she's young wide-eyed and genuinely likes me for whatever reason. She sees something passed my broken wires. I wouldn't swap her company for anyone else's. If I had to go on the longest journey I'd save a seat for her. I think we should be together. I want to feel what a life with her feels like. I think she would make me human. I want to know what that's like.

Poem:
Wearing black

Black is the colour of my emptiness, my room with the lights off. On her, black is a long flowing dress. A sky that hangs around one star. We're both in black with skin the shades of brown and vanilla.
We wear our colour every day. Hers reaches the ground from her head. Mine reaches the last depths of my heart from the caves of my mind.
Walking by me she brings a sunrise with her over my black turning it into rays of reds, oranges and yellows. Making me the colour of daylight.
So when they say we can't be together because I'm black and she is not. I say to them she wears black for her Lord and the Lord made me black, for her

ABOUT THE AUTHOR

Zak Aadam was a solitary black child, raised on the winding path of Atherfold road Clapham, South London. His birth right would be British but his blood would flow with Jamaican black, yellow and green. Without a father, brother or sister he has survived the dark and the turmoil's of youth to reach a poetic maturity. Christianity and rap music made the background for his soul but he would come to the light of Islam, and practice the Deen in 2014 by the Docks in South East London. Zak Aadam has a degree, in Journalism and advertising from the university of West London and published his first book, A Solitary Black in 2015.